Outspoken

True Colours

First published in 2021 by True Colours.
All poems © True Colours 2021.

Contents

Culture Clash

I eat chicken on the bone with my fingers

staff look at me and their stare lingers

because I'm not using a fork

or eating pie of pork

or ham and cheese

oh please stop

before I make a police stop

and arrest you mid stare

personally, I don't care what you think

but tell me again my food stinks

I'll be up in your grill like toast

make you feel most unwelcome

but I really want to educate and help them

because our backgrounds are different

I eat different food for instance

but that doesn't give you the right to tell me it's disgusting

carry on and I'll be thrusting it down your throat

you'll see its nice

by the way its Jellof rice

a staple west African dish

yes, it can contain fish

but its cooked to taste

guaranteed none goes to waste

but I'm going off course here

there is a lesson of course here

don't knock it till you've tried it

if you don't want to, keep quiet

think before you speak nonsense

if cultural knowledge was money, you'd have one pence

when you go on holiday or live, in countries like Spain

the locals think you're a pain

every night you order steak and chips

then get pissed

shake those hips with fellow Brits

dancing to Shakin Stevens

speak fast for no reason

don't try to appease them

don't want to learn the language

yet you're telling the Spanish waiter in English all your

anguish

and he can't understand half of it

there lies your problem

well part of it

because you want to live British abroad

get dead fat, call yourselves ex pats

when foreigners live here, they're called immigrants and

abhorred for your angst

when in fact you should give thanks

because without them the UK would look sucked

if you don't believe me you can go and get ffffff' hooked

on the world wide web

read instead of listening to tarnished views

from BBC news

that lean awkwardly to the right

you watch cautiously through the night

getting hypnotised by biased mantra

with so many additives it may as well be Fanta

though there's nothing sweet about it

with bitterness you tweet about it

for hundreds to read

and hundreds agree with you

because not much is going on in their lives

having marital problems with their husbands or their wives

getting laid off at work

they need to go berserk

but nobody ever blames the English boss who hired them

cheap labour, hmmm I wonder what inspired him

what a joke

foreigners, please take note

you will be blamed for most things

while the same people are boasting

about their Japanese sports car

sipping German beer in a sports bar

posting pictures of the Indian curry they're about to eat

you see its all deceit and lies

there are such tenuous ties

that separate us

just to desecrate us

and keep us from being one

so, power to the people there's none

we are categorised and separated

so togetherness is decimated

into colour, race, creed and class

which evolves into one big culture clash.

Snowflake

To compare certain humans to a snowflake

is an insult to the flake and the snow

the snowflake isn't a flake for the show

a snowflake is integral to creating that huge mean feat

beneath our feet

tread carefully or you'll get swept off your feet

if you think a snowflake is weak

your winter of contempt will be bleak

the snowflake is mighty in numbers

never wanders

once it has found its residence

the snowflake sticks together and sets precedence

cool under pressure

depending on whether the weather

is made to measure

the snowflake is very clever

and adapts to its surroundings

unlike the human snowflake

the snowflake remains cool and very well grounded.

Just Banter

You use the word banter

like a kid at Christmas, saying Santa

in its present state

I hate that word

because you will say something mad offensive

then say it is just banter

like you don't know what the offence is

banter is now your cliche

he says she says thinking you are funny

poorly disguising your prejudice

with the incredulous

proverbial banter

where's your banter gone when you are not with your clones

your banter dissipates amongst different mates and

different tones

not playing to the crowd now are we?

to get a cheap laugh like Dad's Army, usually so brash

aren't we?

happy playing the clown

happy playing to your common crowd

with weak vocabulary and limited nouns

licking each other's ass

for cheap laughs and back slaps

picking on the odd one out

no doubt

so unoriginal

not even intelligent enough to be subliminal

or geographically accurate

you apparent parrot

you're too daft to own up

so, let me give you a good tone up

did that hurt? it's just banter

and it's for your own good.

Smartphone Idiot's Hand

Smartphone in an idiot's hand

pays extortion for an idiot brand

some stand in the queue for hours

patiently waiting for the patient with flowers

using their current phone to take a farewell selfie

stealthy

in the zombie's queue

to get their idiot hands on a smartphone anew

the latest gimmick comes with it

"what you going for?" he replies "unlimited in it"

unequivocal gimmicks

used for this chat, social media and that

it's the fact that

this seems to be the be all that ends all social interactions

by so many fractions

so much affirmative action for a certain distraction

there is a certain attraction

that I get yet lest we forget the debt

to murder and slave labour

from so long ago

till now in the Congo

it's wrong though

I am part of the problem

if you do not know research Tantalum it comes from Coltan

the Belgian's king Leopold and co devised the whole plan

Europe benefiting 'til this day

while they portray Africa in disgrace

when it should be the other way

England only tells you one side when its two faced

the phone is so smart it will barely leave your side

while you brag about the latest slightly different new edition

with pride

while your old, new phone will still suffice

you pay for an upgrade for a ridiculous price

they bring out new toys

of course, you must have them

so, you grab them

update apps and add them

to the list of meaningless shit

smartphone in an idiot's hand

sad thing is I do apply to some of this

smartphone in an idiot's hand, well, I guess I am it!

More to Me

I am labelled a refugee in this self-proclaimed land of
opportunity
where some lack the spirit of community
although I am a qualified GP, they just see a refugee
when there is a lot more to me
I do not feel the unity, this is all new to me
they say it's the first world yet they don't put the world first
they told us they are the best, but I see worse
I am averse to the verse of cursed words
go back to where you came from
where is your name from? what you are doing here?
why don't you drink beer?
you're stealing our jobs "I can't stand you lot"
I have lost my individual status
they generalise all as one and berate us, we, me
community I have not seen lately
I am misunderstood yet my intentions are good
I still get chastised with hateful eyes
I see the way they receive and deceive me
what happened to being equal
they don't care about the evil I have been through
the atrocities I have seen too

they have never seen the places I have been to

images embedded in my mind I try to erase them all the time

I am not a refugee I am a human seeking refuge

how can fellow human beings be so mean

I mean I have never hurt them personally

nor am I here as mercenary

I feel like it is them versus me I just want to live in peace

not live in pieces I escaped from a place unsafe

to seek safety so do not hate me

I am not your enemy I would like you to be a friend to me

I am a human being who happens to need refuge

so please, refuse me your pity I want to make the most of

this city

get my family settled my wife makes perfume from petals

makes delicious tea with our iron kettle

we just want to settle

I come from a culture of hard workers

not work shirkers

I work for my family's benefit

I am not here to take benefits to benefit

I just want to live a mundane life

and live life as best I can

that is my only plan to raise my family,

like any good family man

before you see a refugee

14

look at me for me

treat me like your fellow men accordingly

yours sincerely

me a human being not a refugee.

Justice

It's not justice
It just is
a rigged system
to fit them
and give the impression
they're teaching us lessons
well my faith lessens
when I see such injustice
In god we trust
It's
not done much good for us
up till now
So how
do we keep forgiving
when we've never been given
justice or equality
you follow me
but maybe you don't hear me
so let me say it clearly
everybody deserves human rights
unless you're not humane, right
who gives whom the right

to change your plight

and they expect you to do it without a fight

or else you get fined

I'm not going to sit in line

I'm going out to get mine

It is time

to see true democracy

not this hypocrisy

making a mockery out of justice

and you expect us to trust it

and by us, I mean WE

so, I've said my piece

No justice

No peace.

Rap at You

I'm really into rap
not really into crap
I like the way words flow
the way words go together
like birds go together
in a flock
like flats in a block
if you really pay attention
you will see the dimension
and foundation
like math and English
I don't rap or sing this
this is a dedication
to the medication
the education of rap
not the commercial crap
it's a commercial trap
that sends out negative implications
and glorified through renegotiation
in order for records to be sold
labels encourage negativity to be told
so, they are controlled

18

by the system
Talib Kweli you missed him
because he's talking truth to the youth
but who wants to hear that
the powers that be fear that
the power of music
can be for good if they choose it
but that's not what they want
so negative stereotypes are a front
mutton dressed as lamb
deceiving us is their plan
the art of rap is full of grammatical intricacies
tongue twisters and similes
encourages mind improvement
it's not just music it's a movement
has nothing to do with guns
the n word, hoes
bitches, pimps, pros, gold teeth, jewellery
this my friends is tomfoolery, buffoonery
images and sounds of prejudice and stereotype
while you turn your stereo high
and rap along
to a raspy song
don't get me wrong
I was once sucked in

'til one day I got tucked in

to reading and teaching myself

it's all about the label owner's wealth

than the music itself

they abuse it

by selling us fifty by the cent

Nicky Mirage making dents

in the minds of the masses

deceiving young lasses

twerking, jerking, showing asses

throwing their assets down

looking to get down

teenagers idolising troll models

idolising a facade as a role model

not saying they are bad people

I'm saying the balance is unequal

with the amount of negativity portrayed

to the people en mass on blast

realise the real lies in the images displayed

explicit lyrics and images over played

real rap has no business with that

real rap is fun with facts

it paints pictures from the authors of the streets

broadcasting what they can see

story telling mastery

RAP is rhythm and poetry to the beat

bringing the heat from suburbs, street and heart

which sets this art

apart

from commercial garbage

the industry tarnished the image

and aspirations diminished with it

so now we have generations

who glorify gangster, all thanks to

the soul stealers

they broke it down and distributed like dealers

so now you're hooked on crap

and it's hard to get off that

getting caught in head locks

if you stick your head in a stock

they'll throw crap at you

I can see clearly now that reign has gone

so, I had to rap at you.

Costa Coffee Carbon Copy

Sat in Costa coffee

with branded cup filled with overpriced coffee

laptop, phone, with that costa coffee carbon copy look

with a copy of that book

called generic as f@$k

but it's ok because they look good

so their followers tell them

looking for likes propels them

on a daily bread basis

our father who ar...

let's face it

we are doomed to this technological boom

that consumes brain cells

"look at me" is the main sell

the profound will be found in the ground

buried with all the intelligence

that's relevant to stimulate

the so called intelligent

how elegant is the idea of elegance

when one acts, to attract the irrelevant

now the irrelevant has become the so called

relevant

physical attributes precede the spiritual attitude

generic designer brands, fake teeth, fake tan, just bate, man

hence why keeping outside that costa coffee carbon copy box is my plan.

IF I Told You

This time last year if I told you

you'd be on house arrest

unneighbourly relations put to the test

If I told you there'd be football games with no football fans

told you can't work without plans

If I told you

that all bars and pubs will be shut

wages, hours and jobs will be cut

If I told you

you will have so much free time

to stay in wine and dine

wake up at five to nine

drink beer from 9 to 5

to add to that

If I told you

everyone had to wear a mask

as a precautionary act

then to add to that

If I told you

those so-called patriots that scoff halal fast food kebabs

smoke Kurdish tabs

are the same people mad at Muslims for wearing burkas

and niqabs

saying face covering is a security risk

If I told you this

the following year the very same people that cried face

covering is a security risk

are the very same people saying not wearing face covering

now is (a security risk)

If I told you this

you'd call them fickle hypocrites

you'd be like what kind of twit is this

you'd be telling me I'm taking the piss

If I told you this

you'd look at me like I'm daft

you'd say I'm a mad man

you'd say "this country could never get that bad man"

If I told you this

you'd get dead defensive

much less pensive, there would be much laughter at my

expense

you would never have it

you truly wouldn't want to hear it

you'd call me a conspiracy theorist

If I told you this

that when all this happened nobody did knish

to stop it

If I told you

we are to blame for how it's going

the contradictory nature and conformity to

such terms is flowing

through subservient veins

If I told you

It'll never go back to being the same

you'd probably never look at me the same

you'd probably never talk to me again

for the simple fact you'd think I'd probably lost my sane

If I told you

we had several warnings

and we've ignored it

If I told you all this

you'd think, crazy, thick or sick

If I told you this

is actually happening now and you're ok with it

Imagine I told you all this

I can imagine you'd say what sad stupid dumb wits

would be so compliant to this?

End SARS

I see my friend's scars
a desolate reminder
that the past is never behind you
brutality on the streets
murders and beats
in the name of some kind of law
and some kind of order
that's out of order
lawless thugs
got the power bug
killing people
this is nothing short of evil
police brutality
like its America the sequel
while we are overseas
being overseen trying to be seen as equal
you guys are giving the western world reason
for the racist narrative to appease them
to say look how bad it is
you know that old narrative
"black on black crime"
we hear it all the time

when your skin shines like ours

footage is shown for hours

of cowards killing the innocence

callous with no inner sense

the time is imminent

to end SARS with immediate effect

let it never resurrect its ugly head

under a different name

stop going out to extort, kill and maim

yes Nigeria you're to blame

but I know you're much better than that

as a matter of fact

yet now you're exploiting human beings

you're making an ugly scene

In such a rich & beautiful nation

to disgrace yourself in such devastation so blatant

following in the Oyibo footsteps

when you should pave your own with good steps

Nigeria, end SARS for good

or you shall forever be tarnished with this stain

you will only have yourself to blame

please don't disgrace yourself to the world again.

SARS is Nigeria's Special Armed Robbery Squad. End SARS fights against police brutality and corruption in Nigeria.

Simple Minds

You think racism is a dying breed
but racists don't die in breeds
they raise and breed
racists planting the seed
of hatred to their offspring
they pass on the baton and off they spring
funny how clothes become dated
yet racism is never outdated
like graffiti in the 80s
finding different ways to paint it
abstractly but still just as matter of fact
desperate to hold onto an identity that is purely fabricated
through fact less visuals
out of touch with their spiritual
they pick a literal side
with misguided pride
then ride the flag of misplaced hate
while common sense is scarce and sacred
morality has been overtaken
replaced and forsaken
which is why such simple minds are there for the taking.

Comment Haters

The easiest thing to do is dismiss others and moan

while you're sat there at home

holding your phone alone

because you are a warrior of the keyboard

to make so much effort you really must be bored

filled with so much anger and rage

we see you all over the comment page

you see an article or comment you don't like you can't

wait to commentate

the one thing you all have in common is common hate

with your non thought-out rhetoric

not one original positive comment

so many cliches

so many he says she says

you all sound like you're reading from the same page

and script

yes, you who's getting angry at this

currently typing away to this

mid red mist

you can't wait to blurt out

30

so daft and desperate you miss words out

the common comments of hatred set adrift

by a set of twits

ten a penny in the comment section

do you lack that much attention?

do you really need a mention?

do you actually read what the article is about?

before you engage your brain and open your mouth

our aim is to shed light

not to spread hate or cause fights

why does another person's plight

make you so impolite?

is that how you were raised?

is that how you teach your children to behave?

at home or in public

is that the path you pave?

making such ignorant hateful comments it's disgusting

just because you had a different upbringing and experience

you can't compare yours to theirs on hearing it

a female doesn't know how it feels to be male

like a male doesn't know what it's like to be female

it's all about attention to personal detail

it's nothing like the pitiful examples you regale

that's why it's important to listen to each other and learn

we listen to each other and earn

knowledge is power

instead of being sour

be sweet about taking in another person's point of view

learn something you never knew

it's so easy to rave and rant

but how would you feel if that bad thing happened to

your aunt, your son, daughter your brother, your mate,

your mother, your dad

wouldn't you feel bad?

wouldn't you feel sad?

seeing comments that others were glad

doesn't that make you feel embarrassed for humanity a tad?

does it make you feel better seeing others in pain?

from your nasty comments what do you actually gain?

if you've got nothing good to say stay in your lane

all we ask you to do is use your brain open your eyes

try to empathise

try to look at things from the other side

why not try and well-wish

instead of being so selfish

why does it make you so mad

are you really that pathetically sad

that you can't even sympathise

are you that detached,

that desensitised?

or is it because it's you being described

the archetypal generic Mr or Mrs I'm not racist

or misogynistic so simplistic how ironic

or are you just jealous, if so just tell us

because your comments are selfish, sexist or racist

you're clearly angry at life let's face it

it must be that bad you want others to suffer

we are all human beings all sisters and brothers

we don't have to get along to live on this earth

we don't get long to live on this earth

so why waste time acting your worst

try putting yourself in another person's shoes

how would you like people to treat you?

if you don't really understand, just listen

opening minds is my mission

whether black, brown, white, straight gay or transgender

peace and equality is the agenda

I just want to raise awareness

I just want you to stop being careless

so that everyone is treated with fairness

so if all of the above annoys you

I truly feel sorry for you

if you're one of those people who likes to be abhorrent

be original for once in your life

and leave a positive constructive comment.

Set Sea

She only saw me for me
her mates would make a mockery
saying how could you date one of me, one of them
this came from her apparent friends
she naively thought they thought like her
thoughts of their prejudice had not occurred
until they realised her boyfriend was black
to her it was not a fact of any matter
as a matter of fact
they did not concur
keeping it white is what they prefer
refer to her as black meat
then see me, meet me, greet me
having no inkling I know of their deceitful ways
of which I hate, but must 'play the game'
she held so much back to protect my back
"I didn't think your boyfriend would be black"
"why did you go and do that?"
"now you are going to be known as baby spice because
you are damaged goods"
you are going to get hurt and damaged good
"he's gonna break you in two"

"he's gonna cheat on you, all black men do"
"you know they are partial to domestic violence too"
"STDs so many of them do
you better go for a checkup you"
"he does look a bit of a thug, I bet he sells drugs"
"did I tell you they are partial to get violent?"
all this time she is silent
keeping quiet while emotions run riot
drained and tired she cries in private
people making her love feel like it is a sin
are the people actually committing the sin
all because, of the colour of my skin
she said she wanted to tell me but did not know where
to begin
all these years later she opens up
like an open book
she relays to me in detail
all the barbaric racist regale
merely because she dated a black male
she was emotionally blackmailed
to leave me
set sea and sail.

IF I Was White

Personally, if I was white, I would always believe everything
the news told me
I would be less empathetic as an old me
I'd probably think everything was alright
I'd tell you to stop going on
I'd tell you where you were going wrong
if I was white
I'd probably get my ass out
on a night out
I'd get white boy wasted 'til it's lights out
I wouldn't think or care about how you viewed me
seeing innocent black people killed wouldn't move me
if I was white
I wouldn't care about or understand Black Lives Matter
I'd probably say all or white lives matter
go around ripping down posters and banners
if I was white
I'd tell you to get some manners
I'd tell you about your bad attitude
I'd say you were aggressive and rude
If I was white
I'd think I know more than I did

I'd cuss him like an adult when he's just a kid

I'd ask where you from?

then ask you where are you really from?

I'd assume you have a baby mum or more than one

if I was white

I'd say p!#i shop instead of shop

instead of saying you guys I'd say you lot

if I was white

I'd avoid talking to any black people about race

I'd have a token black mate touch his hair and grab his young

looking face

he would be the butt of my unoriginal jokes

then tell him when he got upset chill out mate it's only a

joke

if I was white

I'd be blissfully unaware of different ethnicities

because they all look the same to me

when you accuse my mate of being racist

I'd defend him to the hilt and say, but he's not racist

if I was white

I'd say you can't say anything nowadays

I wouldn't see the error of my ways

I'd ask you why can't I say the n word

how come it's ok for black guys to use them words

if I was white

I'd be one of those racist cowards on twitter

all twisted, miseducated and bitter

I'd definitely accuse you of playing the race card

when you accuse me of racism my face would jar

if I was white

I'd get pissed off at this poem

I'd be like f this I'm going

I'd pull faces and make remarks behind your back

I'd say you only got that because you're black

if I was white

I'd say we are alright

you lot are the problem stealing our women and get into

fights

I would never admit my prejudice

if you tried to school me I'd be incredulous

if I was white

I'd never disown my racist friends

I'd tell you he didn't mean any offence

I'd never date outside my ethnicity

I wouldn't even date someone outside my city

if I was white

I'd say I don't find black people attractive

I'd tell you that like it was nothing drastic

if I was white

I'd really love defending Liam Neeson and John Terry

but say I'm not racist cus I fancy Halle Berry

if I was white

I'd get really angry at you saying that white people can be

really racist

then I'd get even more angry and be really racist

if I was white

I would be defiant and belligerent

and even when you told me the error of my ways

I would walk away still blissfully ignorant.

Outspoken

I must be Outspoken
in this gesture token society
where showing face is priority
being seen to be doing the right thing
the writing's on the fall
because we are always head down texting
virtually connecting, we are virtual collections
with more of a lesser connection
repetition is a lesson that lessens
our ability to be vociferous
they have figured us out
not long ago you could say no
today they say stop then you can go
when they say so
like monopoly we are monopolised
with a lot of fines a lot of times
it's the fine of the times
with a lot of fine lies
on top of lies
so I've got to be that guy
Outspoken till the day I die
I

simply point out the obvious

that many are oblivious to

Noah's ark animals came in twos

humans come in crews

feed off the news and off they spew

don't be that lad or lass that follows fads

pave your own path

release that mask

let's weave together like baskets

don't hide the truth like the law and mask it

strive to be better and go past it

be Outspoken

otherwise, there's no hoping

rope a dope tactics makes a dopey bloke practice

absorb it like smoke

your silence must be broken be Outspoken

when the system's deliberately broken

millions of mouths open, hoping

waiting for blow back

deluded idiots thinking they can tell me to go back

when I was born here they need to know that

and even if I wasn't you have no right to tell anyone to

go back

I'm Outspoken and I will expose them and that

in writing or speech, lets teach

those queuing to be spoon fed, soon fed,

soon led, writing is on the wall

you'll be pencilled in for medicine

oh dear oh dear like venison

you're fair game to the insane

hunting for your brain

for an exchange

to make change out of you

till there's no change out of you

we are the power they are the few

who knows what we, together can do

all I know is the more we listen and give

the more we get

the more we sit

the more we let

the more we get played

like arcade tokens

stand up and don't just slot in

show Your True Colours

and be Outspoken.

About True Colours

I started True Colours Clothing a couple of years ago. The idea behind it was to be more than just attire. It's about being true to yourself, not following the crowd, embracing individual and cultural differences and acceptance over tolerance.

Growing up as black British I have been the victim of racism both from peers and institutionally. There was always an underlying pressure I put on myself to try and fit in, which a lot of the time went against my upbringing and morals. In my impressionable years it led me into some very precarious situations hanging around with people I shouldn't have been, due to fear of being isolated, picked on and left out.

After working for the best part of 20 years with young people I decided to start my own enterprise incorporating the ethos of (True Colours) SYTC into workshops, which I facilitate in colleges, youth provisions and PRUS around the Midlands and South Yorkshire. The program consists of a series of topics such as mental health, peer pressure, bullying, racism, xenophobia, knife crime and what it takes to make it.

I encourage everyone to show their True Colours.

www.showyourtruecolours.co.uk

@true_colours_clothing_official

Big love to my Mum and Dad for creating, raising and guiding me the way they did. If it wasn't for them, I wouldn't be who I am now. They taught me to not stay silent, to not let things build up and to challenge things. I can't thank them enough for that.

Also, thanks to Martin Grey (@martingreypoet) for helping me edit this book. I couldn't have done it without him. Go check out his book The Prettyboys of Gangster Town.

Printed in Great Britain
by Amazon

78254601R00031